The Old Scraggly Tree

Bobby Brunson

ISBN 979-8-88540-511-9 (paperback)
ISBN 979-8-88540-512-6 (digital)

Christian Faith Publishing
832 Park Avenue
Meadville, PA 16335
www.christianfaithpublishing.com

Printed in the United States of America

INTRODUCTION

I'd like to share a poem the Lord has placed in me
About a story that happened long ago, apparently.
So come with me on a journey by lending an ear,
And let's imagine turning back the clock to yesteryear.

Oh, a million pardons, my manners are very few.
Let me introduce myself as I share my tale with you.
I've only taken for granted that you can surely see
By my distinct appearance, I am but an old scraggly tree.

Youth is gone, and wisdom has made me quite old and gray,
And little nourishment has taken its toll, I would say.
Many of my branches have withered and are now dead,
And roots have rotted for lack of water—or age, instead.

No one is really to blame for my uncomely sight.
It was by way of the wind, as a seedling I did light
On this rocky soil above the Jericho road,
Between Jerusalem and Bethany is my abode.

Though I'm just a lowly piece, I really can't complain.
There are some advantages being on this lofty plain.
You can just see for miles, and the view is quite serene.
The air is crisp and clouds—the most beautiful you've ever seen.

My friends are the wind and the raven on a sunny day,
And at eve, the stars reach down, twinkling and wanting to play.
As the moon breaks o'er the eastern hills, all glimmery,
If I really stretch, I can almost discern the Salt Sea.

If you only had the time, I'd share many a tale,
And I know I'm quite the talker, so I'll only briefly dwell
On perils of weary trav'lers who have waged this road,
Bringing fine linen and spices, exotics by the load.

Of farmers with their harvest and oxen to be sold
And wealthy tax collectors hoarding their purses of gold.
Of passing kings and their kingdoms down through the ages
Leaving their imprint on this land and chronicle pages.

When I was but a sprout, a Macedonian came,
Sweeping down from the north—Great Alexander was his name.
Seleucids and Ptolemies contesting Ares,
And Maccabees rebelling against Epiphanes.

We now have the Romans with "Pax Romana," indeed.
Crimson, gold, in armor, afoot or upon their great steeds.
The voice of oppression cries "Peace" but to no avail.
Tension is so thick you can cut it with a sickle.

Religious sects are in political upheaval.
The Pharisees condemn the Sadducees for their evil,
And the latter shake their bony fingers at the scribes.
Yet all are guilty of selfish piety, greed, and bribes.

The Essenes have left town, claiming to be divinely sent.
Now someone's dipping folks in the Jordan and yelling "Repent."
Heaven only knows what this chaos will finally bring.
Rumor is, another is performing some outlandish things.

THE NAZARENE

The sick are being healed, and cripples are walking.
The blind can now see, and the dumb rejoice for their talking.
And now, they claim a dead man has been raised by this one.
They call him the Nazarene—a common carpenter's son.

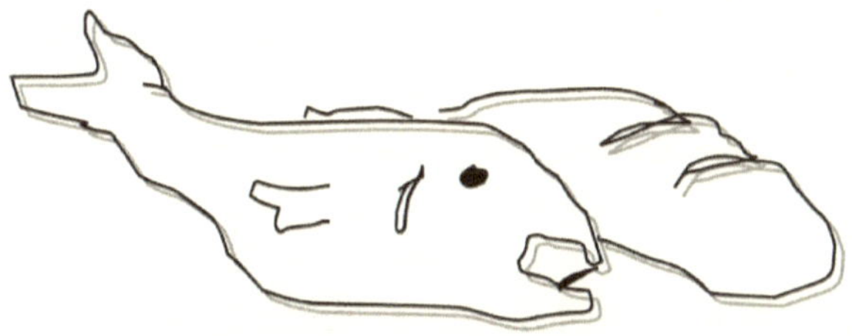

And just the other day, thousands of people were fed
With just a couple of fishes and a few loaves of bread.
By voicing a command, the storm obeys quietly.
No boat does he need nor to swim but walks upon the sea.

Dare we call him "Son of God"? He prefers "Son of Man,"
And the fishers who follow him are now "fishers of men."
People are drawn unto him wherever he may be.
Who is this Master, named Jesus, that all have come to see?

His parables are shared for the people of the land,
Which belittles the devout who claim to have command.
He has placed wisdom in hearts and minds that once were dim,
And yet he even has time for the children who come to him.

He brings to light the mysteries and writings of old,
For he places his authority on what he has told.
He leads the downtrodden, the weary, and those who sorrow
From this world's sin and darkness into a heavenly glow.

The lawyers try to entrap him, but his words prevail,
Which only hardens their stone-cold hearts every time they fail.
He beckons us to enter the straight and narrow gate,
To walk another mile for the soldier we use to hate.

Pray in humbleness, "Abba, Father," and not for show,
And have poverty of spirit while being meek and low.
Be willing to give up your riches for those in need
And then to possess the faith of a little mustard seed.

Be at peace with our brothers as we watch what we say.
We should even love our enemies—and for them, pray!
Be concerned for our neighbors for we'll reap what we sow,
Not to prejudge others but edify as we go.

He tells of a Samaritan trav'ling down the way
Who helped a robbed and beaten man, beside the road he lay.
Down the road from here, a few hundred years ago.
I had already forgotten that—but how did he know?

He claims to be the vine, the shepherd, and, yet, the lamb.
If we follow him, he's promised an eternal kingdom.
We are to seek the treasures of heaven's citadel,
Lest our possessive hearts drag us straight through the gates of hell.

Bearing much fruit, denying oneself, bearing one's cross,
Trying to understand such teaching, I'm at a loss,
For my thoughts spin to comprehend such a man as he,
And so challenge my belief for which he claims to be.

But as I stand here with these confused thoughts, wondering,
Trying to make some sense of it all, deeply pondering,
I hear a crowd coming from where Jerusalem lay
And look to see a man leading them this very way.

THE ENCOUNTER

Those around him are happy and sing so joyfully.
It's no wonder—they're the crippled and blind that used to be.
The glow on their faces shows the change in their being.
Yes, they are the ones who have met the Nazarene.

They pause only at a young fig tree across the way,
To partake of its sweetness and enjoy the brief delay;
But an oath is proclaimed, for no fruit is there to taste.
With disappointment, the man turns to lead them on in haste.

But as he turns, his eyes seem to be drawn unto me.
Any defense I've ever had is completely stripped free.
Absorbed with conviction, I stand humbly before this one;
The very man who claims that his Father made creation.

His face, filled with mixed emotion, gazes at this tree.
His anguish and expressed confusion seem to be for me.
The crowd looks on, bewildered at his obvious pain.
What did their Master see in a tree that caused his mood to change?

He slowly turns and walks away, his spirit broken.
He glances back once more as his eyes flood with compassion.
His disciples follow along trying to discern
The scope of their dear teacher's unquestionable concern.

Here I stand consumed with my own guilt and wretchedness.
The shame that has washed over me, I cannot express.
I glance over, then stare aghast, then in dismay,
For the young fig tree is now withered in death and decay.

The swirling dust from the road engulfs the dismal air,
Which only causes the choked feeling within me to flare.
What kind of man has such an authoritative hand
That with his spoken word, even death follows his command?

Yes, this man is truly who He professes to be,
Not just a prophet but the promised Messiah is He!
But what did He see in me that caused His heart to break?
Does His love even extend to care for an old tree's sake?

As I gaze down the road where the feet of many tread,
The dust cloud veils all but a few bobbing heads.
My core cries out in agony for what I have just seen
And seeks answers for what I've heard; what does all of this mean?

Suddenly, a violent pain shakes me from trunk to limb.
Repeatedly, the sound of an axe echoes through the land.
As darkness comes whirling in and I begin to fall,
I notice the familiar cut of a soldier's apparel.

In this moment of darkness, let's pause, dear listener.
If you know Christ, then a prayer I ask you to offer.
That I have strength and courage to continue this tale
And that its message might live forever and never fail.

THE PASSION

Now with blurred vision, my senses begin to return.
But something is dreadfully amiss, I am soon to learn.
My surroundings have changed—I'm not where I used to be.
And that same Roman soldier is now standing over me.

Intense anticipation is written on his face.
He anxiously tightens the hemp around me that is laced.
Two old planks are what I've been rough hewn to be.
Crisscrossed and roped together—a makeshift cross is my decree!

I spit at the very thought of such a spiteful task,
To support some thief to his bitter end—"Why?" I ask.
Oh, such a humiliating sight for all to see,
Two weather-beaten skeletons—a man and a tree.

The soldier grows restless as the mob approaches.
Voices are hoarse with yelling and curses.
They drag the condemned one up the street
And drop him beside me, here at the soldier's feet.

A bloody mass of tissue is all he seems to be,
Beyond human recognition, beaten so ruthlessly.
A soft sob in his voice, breathed with a forgiving tone,
Then I recognize the tender sound of—the Nazarene!

"Dear Master, what have You done to deserve such a lot?
Where is the peace, kindness, and understanding You sought?
Where's the love, joy, and compassion You taught them to do?
What have You done that they'd want to crucify you?"

"By the jeers of the crowd, the accusation is made
That You're King of the Jews—for this, You've been so cruelly flayed?
And You've been crowned with a wreath of thorns—with evil done.
Dear God, reach down and help Him if He truly is Your Son."

But He's roughly jerked up, and I'm laid across His worth.
My weight is too burdening, causing Him to sprawl in the dirt.
A Cyrenian is yanked forward to serve in the ordeal,
And the brutal procession heads on to Golgotha hill.

Upon reaching the summit, with hatred everywhere,
Voices reach a frenzy as eyes gleam with malicious terror.
I'm cast to the ground, and the accused is placed on me,
And a fragile wrist is pinned to wood by a heavy knee.

A Roman steps forward with the objects in his hand,
The very instruments that strike a chill right where you stand
And cause a hush on lips while nervous eyes glance around,
Seeking reassurance in what is about to be done.

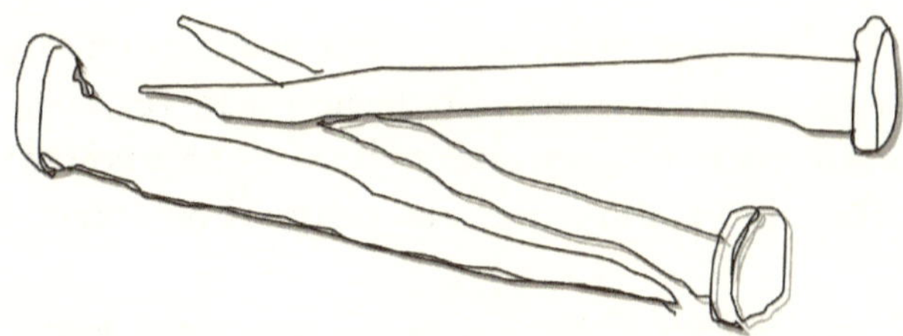

The silence is now shattered by the thunderous blow
Of vicious steel being rammed thru flesh and wood with echoed toll.
Winceful eyes keep time as the hammer swings relentlessly,
Harmonized by the piteous wails of a man and a tree.

Being hoisted on end and my base dropped into a hollow,
Causes hemp to tug at wood as flesh tears against metal.
Dirt is kicked in around my footing to truss our worth,
And thus, we crudely hang halfway between heaven and earth.

As the hours drag by, the throngs slowly dissipate,
Having grown tired or bored with death in travailing wait.
A man's soul hanging in the balance of life and death,
Placed between two thieves—tries to grasp another wheezing breath.

The stench of clotted blood has thickened the atmosphere,
While mocker's spittle dangles from our humility bare.
Swollen lips, parched by the sun, attempt the word, "Water,"
But are only rewarded by the taste of vinegar.

My limbs ache from the terrible load, which is innate,
Compared to the soul shouldering an even greater weight.
A heart of compassion for a world that's gone awry,
"Dear God, show your mercy on this one who's about to die."

In my despair, I feel my grip slipping from this man,
As He slowly grows limp within my grasp to a certain.
"Dear Master, please, please hold on—don't let it end this way.
Heavenly Father, send your angels to bear Him away."

The sky begins to darken, though an afternoon sun,
An uneasiness creeps into the hearts of everyone,
For the eerie stillness seems to blanket the unknown.
No one breathes as panic crouches to pounce on wicked bones.

A sudden clap of thunder uncoils from deep within.
The ground shakes, rocks break, men grovel in the dirt for their sin.
The very gates of hell seem to break forth and about,
And over it all, "It is finished!" a lone voice cries out.

Deadness…lies heavy on most inner of the soul
As men sink in shame having completed their savage goal.
A man's blood has been shed as payment for men's hatred.
Oh, what have we so cruelly done in our fit of vengeful dread?

A soldier places his sword to Jesus's side, then thrusts,
And curses when he's drenched by the blood and water that burst.
Oh, wretched vultures, cursed wolves leave us in peace.
Let the dead be dead; let vengeance be gone and hatred cease.

Dear Joseph of Arimathea and Nicodemus,
With compassion, remove this crumpled body of Jesus.
Carefully wash and wrap it in clean linen and myrrh.
Place Him in a tomb, for with the dusk, the Sabbath enters.

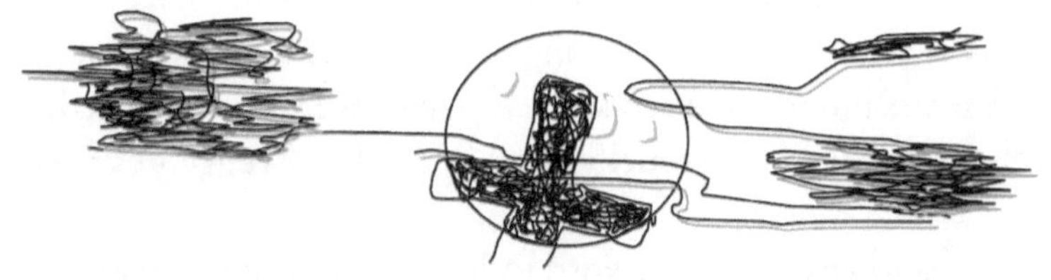

THE SABBATH

In this darkened hour, all alone in my despair,
There is no one to relieve me of the pain I bear.
This awful memory shall haunt me forevermore.
Oh, what I would give for the youthful days I had before.

But all my life, I've been just a worthless piece of wood,
Never sprouting a blossom or bearing seeds for the good.
And now, I've helped to kill God's holy and righteous Son.
Oh God, be merciful and forgive me for what I've done.

That sad day on the road, when He stood and looked at me,
His heart broke, for He knew then what I would come to be.
Only the Son of God could see the nature within.
Yet He showed love and compassion for an old rough wooden.

And now, I've crucified the one that came to give peace.
Will this world forever suffer His untimely release?
Will this sad and darkened Sabbath eternally reign,
As the day the warmth of a life-giving Son died in vain?

Will the birds cease their singing and flowers never bloom?
Will laughter of children and merriment see their doom?
Will the stars, bleak, regain their sheen and come to play?
Will there, again, be fluffy clouds that come to bright my day?

I pray that this cross not spell the destruction it has wrought
And let not the world hate me for what I've brought.
I'm an old wretched stick, and I've killed Your only Son.
Do with me what You will, but bring life back to creation.

I wish away this blackness with all its guilt and shame,
But save us, by Your gracious love, from the eternal flame.
"Lord, can't You just put everything in its rightful place
And forgive us, I plead, by showing Your wondrous grace?"

THE RESURRECTION

The approaching dawn shows dim red over to the east.
With rustling foliage, a breeze seems to bring inner peace,
And the distant coo of a dove echoes what I feel.
Are these symptoms of answered prayer—can I believe it's real?

I feel a low rumble in the ground from somewhere deep,
As if the earth was yawning after a troublesome sleep.
A low groan—the sound of some thwarted and mournful beast
Having watched its guarded captive be unchained, then released.

Then I see it through the trees in the garden below.
There it is, again—something's there—a flicker, then a glow.
Someone's coming—could it be the death angel I see?
What was it I prayed or said to bring God's wrath upon me?

Nowhere to hide from this awful fate imposed,
I can't bear to watch as my sentence is disclosed.
My frame trembles in fear as my judgment comes then.
But I feel, instead, a touch that could only be from the Nazarene!

He gently lifts me up and wipes away my tears
And fills me with a joy that will last a million years.
He wraps me in the warmth of His shining Deity
And encompasses me with eternal serenity.

All the torment that I felt has suddenly taken flight,
As His penetrating brilliance chases away the night.
Oneness with the Savior floods me with radiance;
I've been blessed with the precious grace that only God grants.

He tells me why He gave up His life on this old cross;
The shed blood of the sacrificial Lamb became the cost,
Payment for the sins of a hopeless and dead world.
A Father gave His only Son…with arms unfurled.

And then asked to embrace us with His wondrous grace.
So this old blood-stained cross can now stand with no shameful trace
But proudly say that Christ has won the victory
And the empty tomb—a promise to live eternally.

Our Lord has since ascended to the Father to stand,
But He's sent his Holy Spirit to lend a joyous hand;
He comforts and reassures us of the promise blessed
That Jesus is coming back to take us to heaven's rest!

THE COMMISSION

A good friend of mine recently came by,
Proclaiming good news, the wind had to sigh!
He shared what he just saw on the Jericho road,
In the rocky soil—a stump—my former abode.

A fresh underground spring broke forth during the quake.
It now waters those thirsty old roots, causing them to wake.
A young shoot has sprouted from that old trunk—a remnant,
For God has issued, for His people, a new covenant.

That young shoot shall grow to be strong and bear blossom,
And the wind shall carry its seed throughout Jerusalem,
Judea, Samaria, and the ends of the earth,
Its message—planted in the hearts of men—to seek rebirth.

A father shall tell his child and that son—do the same,
How a loving Father gave His Son to a world untamed.
Generations continue to spread God's Holy Word.
Down through the ages, it's the greatest story ever heard!

Even today, His message has that same great power.
The precious blood of the Lamb covers our sins in this hour,
Which allows our Lord to have sweet communion with us
As we humbly place our hearts and lives in His holy trust.

Dear listener, if you have never heard this story
How Jesus, the Son of God, left His kingdom in glory,
How He came—how He died—for you and for me,
That He has conquered sin and death so that we might go free.

He's preparing a place for us—a heavenly home,
And one day, He's coming—to take us there—no more to roam
And to live forever in the Savior's holy light,
To drink from that river of life with glorious delight!

Is there something knocking at your heart's door—asking in?
Is an emptiness crying out to be filled from within?
It's Jesus calling—bidding you to let Him enter
And to allow His Holy Spirit to fill your center.

It's just as easy as saying, "Yes Lord, please come in!"
Without any hesitation, He will enter right then.
The joy you'll find surpasses all you could ever do.
You can't keep from telling what Jesus Christ has done for you!

Or maybe, you do know the Lord—you can rightly say.
But it has been a while since His blessings have come your way.
"I'm just in a rut," or "God just never talks to me."
Your walk with the Savior seems a little dry and rocky.

Is there something you've kept from Him that you need to share?
It seemed like nothing at the time and no one would care.
Well, it's keeping you from Jesus, so claim it as sin,
And He'll restore the joy of His salvation—a gift from Him.

Perhaps you have kept your eyes on the Lord all these years,
And you have labored hard in His harvest with sweat and tears,
A Sunday school teacher, a deacon, or a trustee,
A hundred committees—the list goes to eternity.

But you feel it's time to let a younger crowd take over.
That rocker on the porch—scratching the ear of ol' Rover.
"Besides, how can God use an old person like me?"
Well, He even had a purpose for an old scraggly tree.

About the Author

Bobby Brunson resides in Portales, New Mexico, with his wife, Kathie. After thirty plus years in the college store industry, Bobby is now retired and spends his time between babysitting grandchildren, leather working, and riding or tinkering on his motorcycles.

He came to know the Lord at a very young age and has aspired to cultivate that relationship throughout his life. While attending Eastern New Mexico University to acquire a Bachelor of Science in two-dimensional design and religion, God inspired Bobby to write the poem *The Old Scraggly Tree*.